OXFORD
UNIVERSITY PRESS

Great Clarendon Street, Oxford, OX2 6DP, United Kingdom

Oxford University Press is a department of the University of Oxford. It furthers the University's objective of excellence in research, scholarship, and education by publishing worldwide. Oxford is a registered trade mark of Oxford University Press in the UK and in certain other countries

Text © Oxford University Press 2023

The moral rights of the author have been asserted

First Edition published in 2023

All rights reserved. No part of this publication may be reproduced, stored in a retrieval system, or transmitted, in any form or by any means, without the prior permission in writing of Oxford University Press, or as expressly permitted by law, by licence or under terms agreed with the appropriate reprographics rights organization. Enquiries concerning reproduction outside the scope of the above should be sent to the Rights Department, Oxford University Press, at the address above.

You must not circulate this work in any other form and you must impose this same condition on any acquirer

British Library Cataloguing in Publication Data

Data available

ISBN: 978-1-382-04341-0

10 9 8 7 6 5 4 3 2

The manufacturing process conforms to the environmental regulations of the country of origin.

Printed in China by Golden Cup

Acknowledgements

The Silver Locket written by Sasha Morton; *A Quest for Riches* written by Jilly Hunt

Illustrated by Paula Zorite, Kate McLelland and Q2A Media Services Pvt Ltd

Author photos courtesy of Sasha Morton and Jilly Hunt

The publisher and authors would like to thank the following for permission to use photographs and other copyright material:

Back cover: MAVRITSINA IRINA / Shutterstock. Photos: p29, 37, 46(a): PA Images / Alamy Stock Photo; p34(bkg), 35(bkg): Wirestock Creators / Shutterstock; p34: Wirestock Creators / Shutterstock; p35(l): The Print Collector / Alamy Stock Photo; p35(r), 46(d): MAVRITSINA IRINA / Shutterstock; p36(bkg), 37(bkg): PA Images / Alamy Stock Photo; p38(bkg), 39(bkg): PietFoto / Shutterstock; p38: Getty Images / Stringer / Getty Images Europe; p39, 46(b): Heritage Image Partnership Ltd / Alamy Stock Photo; p40(bkg), 41(bkg): R A Kearton / Moment / Getty; p41, 46(c): LEON NEAL / Staff / AFP / Getty Images.

Every effort has been made to contact copyright holders of material reproduced in this book. Any omissions will be rectified in subsequent printings if notice is given to the publisher.

In this book ...

The Silver Locket 9

A Quest for Riches 29

ow as in town

oi as in coin

ear as in ear

air as in pair

ure as in picture

er as in otter

ow as in bow

In this book, we see a hidden picture up in an attic.

STOP AND THINK

Can you think of things you might see in an attic?

The Silver Locket

Written by Sasha Morton
Illustrated by Paula Zorite

Fern and Jack hear a low **howl**.

Jack follows Fern up to the attic.

Dark shadows fill the attic.
Jack **shivers** in the cool air.

Fern flips the window shut.

EEK! A person!

Fern **BANGS** into a kit bag.

"Is that an **X** near her foot?" Jack mutters.

Under his own foot is an **X**.

THUD!

They see a silver spark.

Mum appears.

"That is <u>my</u> silver locket!"

Then she sees the picture.

In this book, we go on a quest for hidden riches, such as coins.

STOP AND THINK

Think of things we might spot on the quest.

A Quest for Riches

Written by Jilly Hunt
Illustrated by Paula Zorite

1

A boat is under the soil.
Riches are in it.

silver bowl

gear

TOP FACTS

dug up — 1939

263 things

★★★★★

2

A pot of coins is on a farm. It is hidden in soil.

coin

TOP FACTS

dug up	2010
🧰	52,503 coins

⭐ ⭐ ⭐

37

3

Riches are hidden below a tall hill.

ear clips from a queen

TOP FACTS

dug up	1978
🧰	20,600 things

★★★★★

39

4

Hidden riches are on a farm near a town.

Dig down deeper!

silver bowl

TOP FACTS

dug up 2007

68 things and 617 coins

★★★★

Now look for the riches! Can you see six things?

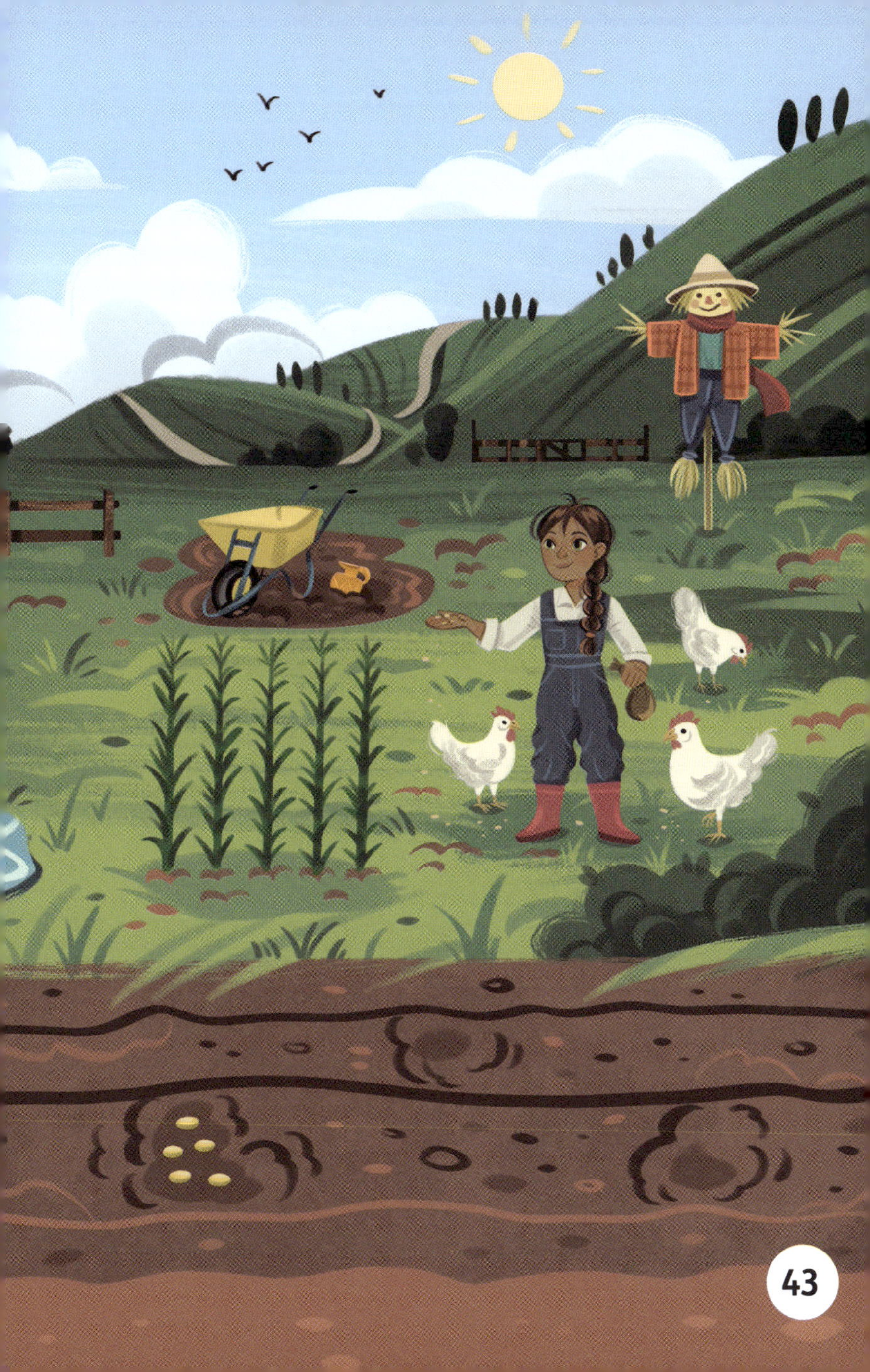

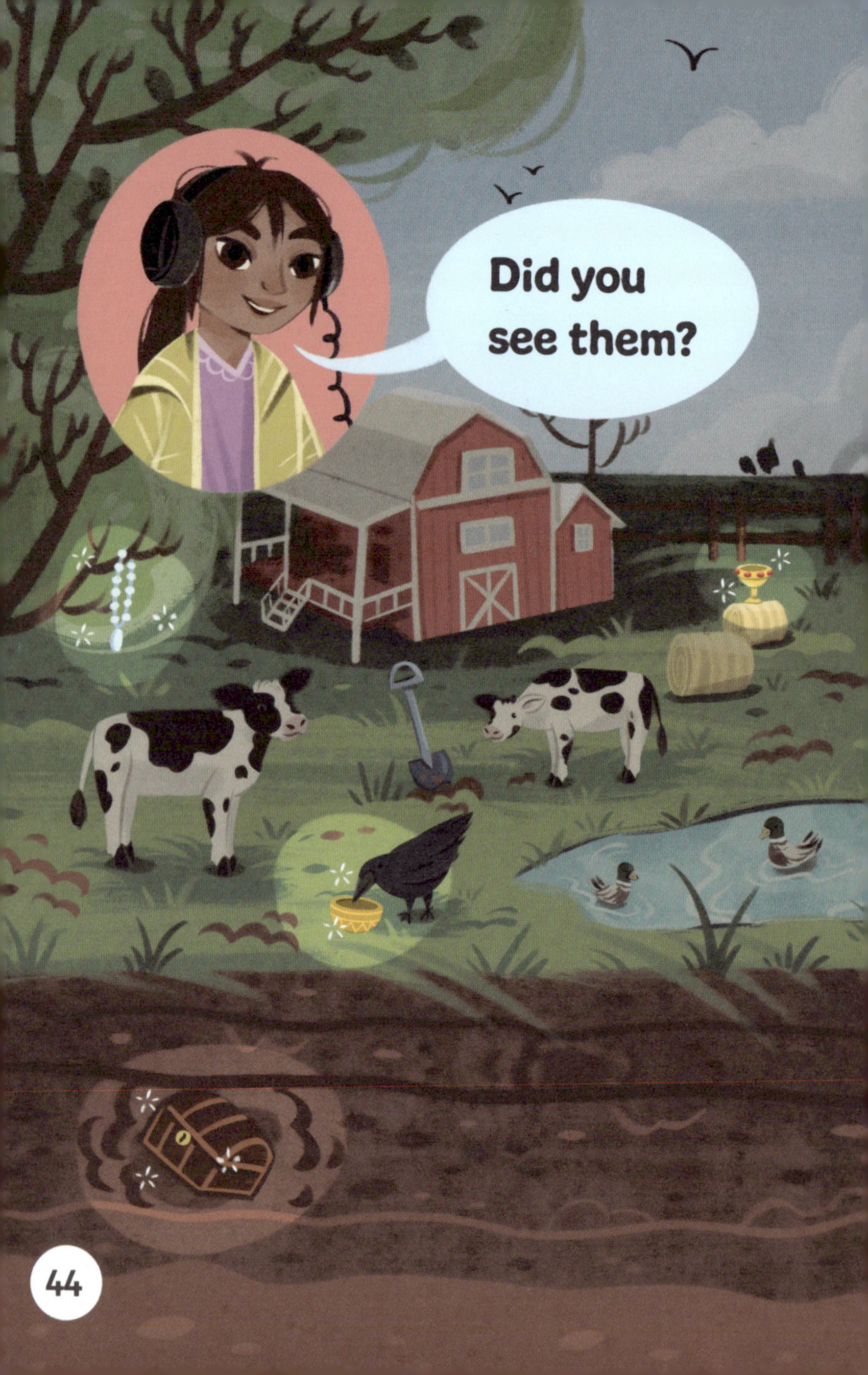
Did you see them?

Link the quest to the hidden riches.

Quest

1.
2.
3.
4.

Riches

A.
B.
C.
D.

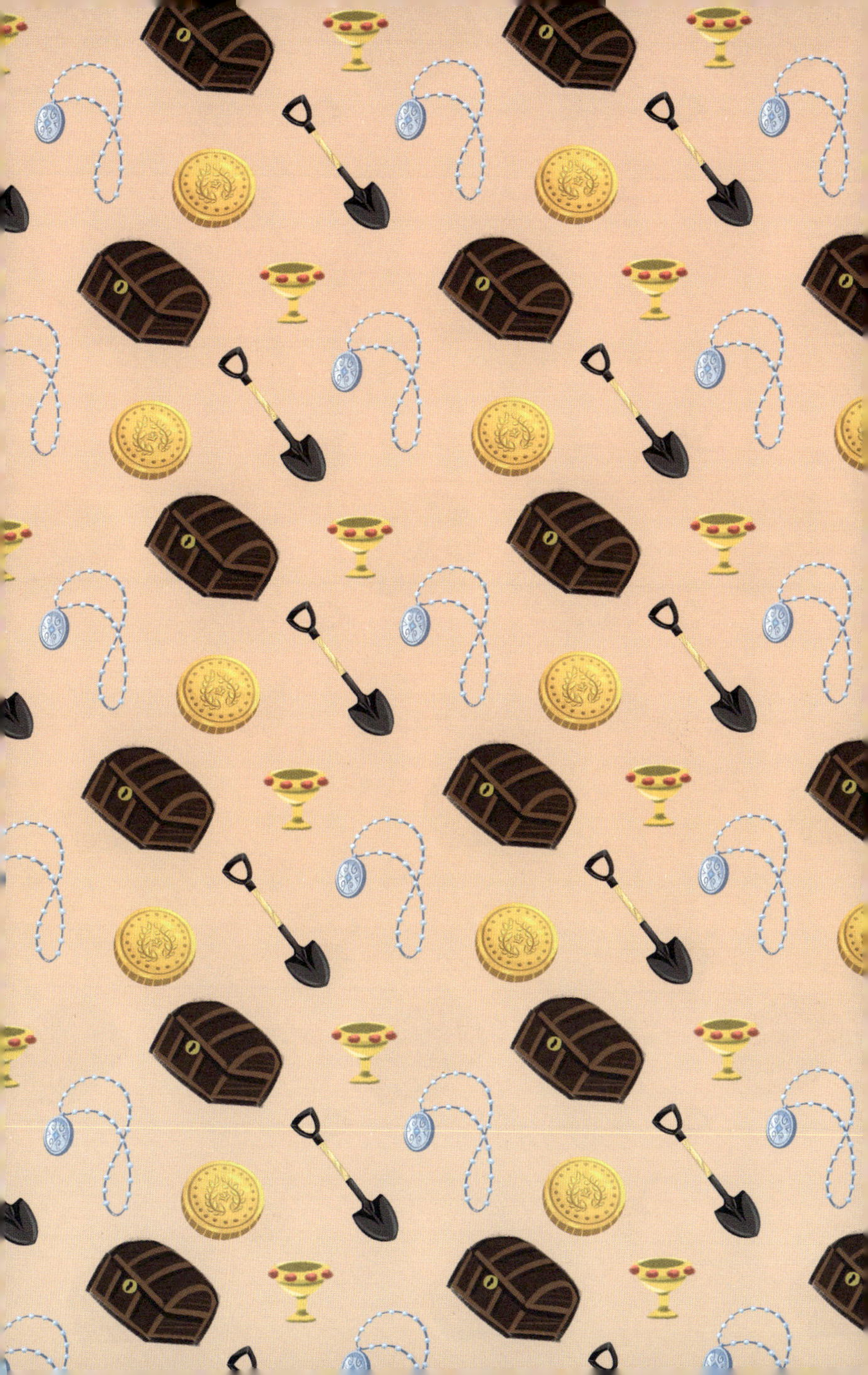